11.50
Amaz Seller

R56216

Over the course of the past two decades the collaborative nature of fashion has been subject to an unprecedented level of attention. Fashion photography, long considered the preserve of celebrity photographers has been analysed to highlight the valuable contribution made by fashion stylists and magazine editors. Similarly, the creative interaction between fine artists and fashion during the last century has been extensively examined through exhibitions, such as the Florence Biennale 97 and Addressing the Century at the Hayward Gallery, London.

Fabric of Fashion focuses on another crucial area of collaboration which has emerged in recent years as a distinctive characteristic of British fashion – the collaboration and in some cases coalescence of the textile and fashion designer. By sharing ideas and working together, the fifteen designers included in this exhibition are fashioning accessories and garments from the inside out, questioning the boundaries between disciplines, challenging assumptions of good design and provoking us to look anew. Asserting the very fabric of their medium, the selected designers in this exhibition seek to re-examine not just the appearance and construction of clothes but other issues too – from environmental and political concerns to highly personal and philosophical ideas. Fabrics, because of the way in which they are produced and the applications for which they are designed, allow these designers freedom to explore a wider range of issues than those offered simply through the conventions of silhouette and style.

Whilst some famous 20th century couturiers are irrevocably associated with their favourite materials – Coco Chanel with soft woollen tweeds and Madeleine Vionnet with matt crêpe – very few of them actually designed and used their own textiles. Issey Miyake's celebrated collaboration with the textile designer Makiko Minagawa however exemplified

that a new creative dialogue could be forged between textile and fashion designer. Together they pioneered innovative methods of fabric construction, promoting a recognition that the only way forward for fashion was to combine craft tradition with sophisticated technology. Many of the designers included in the current exhibition share this view, looking back to traditional craft methods as well as forwards, and to new scientific and industrial applications for inspiration. Although not abandoning their sketch pads entirely, many of their workplaces more closely resemble laboratories than traditional design studios. This is perhaps not altogether surprising given that so many of the designers trained in other disciplines – from sculpture and architecture to biology. Yet despite the diversity in their geographical and educational backgrounds, all of them share an interest in exploring the potential of textiles to develop new forms of expression.

The creativity of the designers selected for inclusion has been parallelled by similar collaborations within the curatorial and design teams responsible for producing the exhibition. From its initial conception through to its final realisation, the curators Marie O'Mahony and Sarah Braddock have combined forces to share skills and expertise in selecting the exhibits and writing the catalogue. In developing the design for the exhibition, the young design team dlm have collaborated with b consultants to fuse the technical and aesthetic process of creative design with manufacture. The fluid organic forms they have designed for the garments not only serve as metaphoric bodies for the works, but mirror the theme of the exhibition. The display system which is an integral part of the curatorial concept for the show breaks new technical ground with a special patented process involving a Lycra-based fabric covered with resin. Working closely together with the stylist Samantha Perry, the photographer

Michael Danner has brought his own
particular vision, informed by a mixture
of documentary and conceptual practice,
to bear on the catalogue photographs.
At the core of the team have been my
departmental colleagues, Louise Wright
and Jo Gutteridge who have maintained
responsibility for coordinating all stages
of the exhibition preparation, catalogue
production and management of the
overseas tour.

This exhibition marks a further stage in
cooperation between the British Council
and the Crafts Council. Having recently
organised the tour of Satellites of Fashion,
initiated by the Crafts Council in 1998,
to the Caribbean and Latin America,
the British Council is delighted to have
an opportunity to extend our professional
relationship with the Crafts Council by
launching the international tour of this
exhibition at their London gallery.

Brett Rogers
Deputy Director
Visual Arts, The British Council

British fashion designers have an international reputation for being eccentric, thought-provoking and boldly innovative. Consistently defying convention, they have put London on the world fashion map for the past forty years. The city itself is renowned for creative dressing alongside traditional fabrics and fine tailoring. Textiles are an essential element and over the past two decades we have seen the worlds of fashion and textile design become increasingly close and reliant on one another. Characterising this practice is a preference for simple, uncluttered shapes which give prominence to the fabric. In creating this unique aesthetic, microfibres, mixes of natural and synthetic yarns and sophisticated finishing treatments are combined with traditional skills. Drawing on examples from the very best British textile design and fashion, this exhibition focuses on the nature of these relationships.

In a world of globalisation, brand names such as Benetton and Levis are omnipresent. They are virtually the same in every country, with occasional colour variations to take account of regional taste. The emphasis is on uniformity, a reassurance that you can look the same as someone in New York, Cairo and Oslo. The British fashion industry has cultivated young designers who have a clear sense of identity and a distinctive creative vision. Their clothes are being worn by those who want to make a statement and be individual. The unconventional is combined with the prim to create a style that is open-minded. British fashion is not prescriptive and people buying the clothes are encouraged to personalise them through the combination of garments and accessories. Unlike global branding, the mixing of different labels is encouraged. The success of this vision can be seen in a recent move by global brand names to offer customisation.

There is no single reason as to why London should have developed this vision; that the city is a cultural melting pot is certainly one factor. This has created a dynamic which means that the city exists in a constant state of flux, both conceptually and geographically. Many of the young designers in this exhibition are based in the East End. The area has traditionally been home to immigrant communities, previously Jewish and more recently Bangladeshi. Each leaves something of their presence when they eventually depart for other areas of the city. This can be seen in the shops, restaurants and even street names. Fashion Street and Haberdasher Street are a reminder that fashion and textile designers are not new to the area.

The development of new materials and technologies has been accompanied by renewed interest in modern couture and craft. British designers draw on diverse sources of inspiration which demonstrate a range of creative ideas and forms of practice. Departure points include the immediate urban environment, the broad world of art and design and visions of the future.

Hussein Chalayan, one of the most creative and conceptual thinkers in British fashion uses unlikely narratives: weather patterns, global communications and portable environments. The avant-garde label, Boudicca (Zowie Broach and Brian Kirkby), often take emotions rather than images or historic costume as their source which they then communicate in an abstract way through clothing. Shelley Fox, who won the coveted Jerwood Fashion Prize in 1999, also pursues a conceptual approach. Her collections have been inspired by geometry, August Sander's photographs and Morse code. British designers are often influenced by cultures other than their own and fashion designer, Tracy Mulligan who has a strong belief in Eastern spiritual philosophies gives each of her collections a title from the i ching. India has played a major role in the work of Nigel Atkinson and his palette of magentas and saffron yellows is inspired by Rajasthan. His attention to surface decoration is often undertaken by Bengali craftsmen who create rich hand embroidery, mirror-work and beading to his designs. Jessica Ogden often uses antique textiles directly in her creation of garments.

Fashion designers understand that the future of their area lies to a great extent in the selection of fabrics. Advanced textile technology has yielded new aesthetics, tactile qualities and performance capabilities. Traditional crafts such as knitting, weaving, embroidery and intricate hand detailing are employed alongside sophisticated new treatments. High technology coatings, laser-cutting and the latest microfibre fabrics, shape memory alloys and technical cloth are all being appropriated from industrial applications. Fashion designers are collaborating with textile designers to produce collections which show innovative fabrics, impeccable craft and attention to detail. Textile designers B. Earley, Eley Kishimoto and Sophie Roet have all created unique fabrics for Hussein Chalayan. Eley Kishimoto started by supplying their textiles to fashion designers and now have their own range of clothing and accessories. They have a look that combines English streetstyle with a Japanese influence – a successful mix which is becoming recognisable world-wide.

Tracy Mulligan works closely with textile practitioners and is interested in hand-craft, texture and strong, graphic printing, stating that "surface decoration is the future of fashion". Her contemporary, minimalist chic gives emphasis to their fabrics with their hand-worked details such as fabric manipulation and embroidery. Textile designer Savithri Bartlett and Boudicca met at the Royal College of Art and have successfully collaborated. Boudicca are interested in unusual, tactile materials and Savithri Bartlett has supplied them with moulded, three-dimensional forms for seamless garments and laser-etched surface decoration. Shelley Fox produces sculptural clothing. Her trademark is hand-felted wool and further experiments include scorched felt and cotton singed with lasers.

Many British designers are mixing aspects of traditional craft with modern technology to create a comfortable, futuristic style. i.e uniform combine the talents of textile designer, Lesley Sealey with fashion designer Roger Lee to demonstrate how craft and technology can merge. "We love to fuse traditional methods such as embroidery with laminates and coatings to create new fabrics". Other designers refer to Britain's textile heritage, keeping tradition alive and imbuing it with a new meaning for contemporary society. Hikaru Noguchi is originally from Japan but now London-based. She reinvents traditional British textile crafts for a look which is classic with a twist using woven Welsh blankets, Fair Isle knits, Shetland and Arran patterns.

Today's British designer is balancing originality of concept with impeccable cutting and craft to create wearable garments, which are provocative and commercially viable. Short-order, small collections or 'demi-couture' and made-to-measure clothing often give emphasis to handcraft and are opposed to the anonymity of mass production. British fashion and textile designers are constantly experimenting and pushing the boundaries of what is expected of them. Unpredictable and thought-provoking, the work of these designers honours tradition while signalling the future.

Marie O'Mahony and Sarah E. Braddock

Nigel Atkinson creates sculptural textiles which are rich in colour, texture and form for use in fashion, accessories and interior. Driven by the fabric and not by fashion trends, his work shows great attention to detail and ideas evolve gradually with variations on a print often being developed over several seasons. Handcraft and traditional textile techniques are used and updated to create contemporary pieces. The end results are classic heirlooms which will be wearable in ten years time.

Atkinson trained at Winchester School of Art, University of Southampton and specialised in Printed Textile Design. It was here that he began hand-printing with Expandex, his trademark. Use of this heat-reactive chemical produces embossed, contoured surfaces which when printed on the reverse of the cloth create complex but subtle reliefs.

Atkinson's work also includes layered and embroidered textiles. He layers up to six lengths which, when cut on the bias give an organic, sensual movement. This enables him to explore contrasts between different hand-dyed colours and various fabric properties, for example, transparency/opacity and softened/stiff textiles. The characteristics of the fabrics complement each other to create malleable, sculptural pieces.

Recently, he has been working with Bengali craftsmen who realise his designs using the traditional techniques of hand-embroidery, mirror-work and beading, crafts which have been passed down through many generations. By using handcraft and aiming his work at the luxury international market he endeavours to keep these traditions alive. Inspiration for his fabrics often originates from antique textiles and the actual age of his work can be ambiguous. In his reference to history he refines the source to convey its essence. Visits to Rajasthan have significantly influenced his palette of garnet, saffron and turquoise.

Atkinson has created textiles for fashion designers including Azeddine Alaïa (his first freelance client) and Romeo Gigli (who commissioned him for five seasons), John Rocha and Alberta Ferretti.

He now produces his own line of garments and accessories which he shows in static exhibitions at London Fashion Week. Silhouettes are simply-cut and stylish, for example, his dressing-gowns and evening coats. In 1994 the Nigel Atkinson Accessories label was established and in 1997 he launched Nigel Atkinson Interior Textiles.

Previous pages, Nigel Atkinson
Fabric detail (1:1) from Sea anemone dressing-gown, 2000
Six tier, hand-embroidered satin organza wrap, 2000

Textile designer, Savithri Bartlett is interested in new technologies, experimenting with nonwovens and laser-etching for fashion textiles.

Born in Sri Lanka, Bartlett came to Britain when she was fourteen. She studied architecture before specialising in textiles at Edinburgh College of Art. Here, she explored printed imagery and woven textiles before investigating the potential of nonwoven fabrics. She continued these studies at the Royal College of Art, London, researching fibres and methods of constructing stable textiles whilst still maintaining a strong aesthetic. Bartlett has challenged assumptions about nonwovens, such as their unsuitability for anything but industrial use and the perception that they are visually uninteresting. Richly coloured samples were produced by needle-punching fibres and applying metallic foil on substrates. Her work was awarded an MPhil in 1997.

In her research, Bartlett has explored the properties of thermoplastic nonwovens. Differences in fabric properties have been assessed with heat-pressed and nonheat-pressed being analysed. She collaborated with Wellman International and Ciba Dyes & Chemicals in creating mouldable, dyed fabrics. On teaming up with mould-maker, Keese van der Graaf, she developed a suitable technique from which moulded, seamless pieces were created. The first commercial work illustrating these investigations were hats for Chanel's Autumn/Winter 1997/98 collection.

Prior to graduating from the Royal College of Art, Bartlett met the fashion design duo, Boudicca and subsequently created fabrics for two of their collections. For Spring/ Summer 1998 - Leave, she showed moulded, nonwovens and Spring/Summer 1999 - Immortality, used her laser-etched fabrics which incorporated text.

She is currently undertaking research towards a PhD at Loughborough University where she is collaborating with the Engineering Department. Use of the electron microscope allows her to examine individual fibres for maximum control over the lasers. Recently, Bartlett has teamed up with Manel Torres who is studying for a PhD at the Royal College of Art.

Boudicca are at the forefront of London's avant-garde and create nonconformist, conceptual couture which comments on contemporary society. Imaginative and inspirational, they create clothing either in small collections or to special commission.

The label Boudicca was formed in 1997 by Brian Kirkby and Zowie Broach. They both trained in Fashion at Middlesex University and Brian Kirkby subsequently studied Womenswear Fashion at the Royal College of Art, London.

Their garments are precision-cut, impeccably tailored and show great attention to detail. Boudicca are interested in materials and have collaborated with textile designers and accessory designers to fulfil their vision.

Manel Torres is currently engaged in PhD research at the Royal College of Art, London. Born in Barcelona, where he trained in Fashion, Torres also studied in Amsterdam before undertaking his Masters degree in Womenswear Fashion at the Royal College of Art. In his work he investigates textile development and production methodologies employing the latest technology and materials which include smart fabrics, polymers and recycled textiles.

Previous pages, Savithri Bartlett and Manel Torres
Fabric detail (1:1) from Laser-cut top, 2000
Laser-cut leather top and hood, 2000

Hussein Chalayan has a conceptual approach to design. He is equally at ease employing the latest technologies, as he is using natural and synthetic fabrics. This may seem like a lot to bring to the design of garments, but the end result has a purity that makes his clothes very wearable.

Chalayan's graduate collection from Central Saint Martins was the now infamous series of buried garments. These had been buried in a friend's back garden, then exhumed just before the show. The work was given the accolade of a window display in Browns. Since then he has worked with a number of designers including textile and product designers as well as architects and artists. The working relationship in each case is different. He collaborated with textile designer Sophie Roet to develop a very fine woven fabric to be used as an overdress with the underdress glowing underneath. The fabric was a double-weave cloth, using polyamide monofilament and cotton yarns. It was finished with a chemical etching process that was a variation on the devoré technique eating away at the cellulose areas. Chalayan has also worked with Eley Kishimoto who designed a pixellated print fabric specially for his Spring/Summer 1996 collection. The design echoed the pixels found on computer images, though in fact the fabric itself was only partially designed on the computer. Flowers were hand-drawn then scanned into a computer to enhance the colour and accentuate the pixellated effect. The very bright colours used in the prints reflect the intensity of the computer's light-based colour.

Not all of Chalayan's collaborations have been with textile designers. He has also worked with a product designer and architects. A series of airplane dresses have been made specially for his catwalk shows, which are maintained for exhibition purposes only. The dresses are made using composite technology more usually associated with the aircraft industry, hence the title of the series. Product designer Paul Topen combined glass fibre and resin, placing them in moulds using a hand lay-up technique. As the name suggests, this involves placing the glass fibres in a mould by hand then pouring resin over it. Once hardened, or cured, the glass fibre and resin material is removed from the mould. The model wears an underdress as protection against the glass fibre and the dress is clipped onto the body using metal clips. A variant of this uses a remote control device to open and close some of the panels on the dress to reveal a frilly pink tutu.

Chalayan's early interest was in architecture which he considered as a career until discouraged by a friend who advised that he would spend his life designing tower blocks and offices. The spatial awareness of an architect's eye is always evident in the relationship between his garments and the body. Forms work with and against the body creating positive and negative spaces. His series of architecture dresses from his Spring/Summer 2000 collection show the continuing influence of architecture on his work. Designed with architectural engineers b consultants, the dresses are printed with wireframe architectural drawings. The images have been computer generated using Microstation software. The programme allows the viewer to move through the architectural landscape and select viewpoints which are then freeze-framed. The frozen images are then transferred onto a fabric printing process and printed on silk and cotton fabrics.

Previous pages, Hussein Chalayan
Fabric detail (1:1) from buried dress, 1995
Two dresses from the Architecture series, spring/summer 2000

The garments and accessories designed by B. Earley are defined by their unique textiles. While designing printed textiles mainly for her own work, she has also designed fabrics for other fashion designers such as Donna Karan, Lagerfeld and Etro. Rebecca Earley uses a special heat photogram printing process, derived from photography, that allows her to use actual objects printed onto fabric at a scale of one-to-one. The result is a ghostly image not unlike an X-Ray in its effect.

Earley began experimenting with the technique while still at college and has been developing and refining it since. She studied both fashion and textiles at Loughborough University College of Art and Design, followed by an MA in Fashion at Central Saint Martins. On leaving college she set up a partnership under the label Earley Palmiero with Giovanna Palmiero, but soon left to concentrate on her own independent label B. Earley. She now produces a range of womenswear, scarves and specially commissioned artworks. The nature of her printing technique means that each piece is in effect a one-off, using a process that she regards as closer to art than fashion.

The fabrics used vary from shiny, satin finish synthetics and reflective fabrics to light-absorbing fleece. The fleece is environmentally friendly, made from recycled soda bottles, more usually used in sportswear. The simple, classical shapes of the garments act as a background for the striking patterns that form a narrative on the fabric. Scarves and wraps are of a generous size and are treated almost like a storyboard with carefully orchestrated objects such as loose knits, lace, herbs and flowers. While utterly contemporary, all of the work is instilled with a memory taken from the imprint of used objects. This is reminiscent of an earlier age where clothes were passed down through generations. These were either clothes for special occasions such as weddings or christenings, or alternatively, clothes that were reused continuously until eventually they became patches of fabric. The patches would find their way onto more recent clothes in need of repair or whole patchwork cushions and quilts. The changing context of a fabric's life is something that underlies much of Earley's working process.

Not all of B. Earley's work is based on imagery taken from used fabrics and garments. Nature is also taken as a subject matter. In 1999, the Queen Elizabeth Centre for the Treatment of Cancer in Birmingham awarded her a public art commission. The commission was to design gowns for cancer patients undergoing treatment. The gowns had to be easy to put on and take off and be more shaped than traditional hospital gowns. Homeopathy was the basis for the printed design using plants with perceived medicinal properties.

One hundred gowns were designed for patients suffering from breast cancer. Each garment was based on a plant or herb with specific healing powers. Garlic and green tea have anti-carcinogenic properties, beet and root vegetables help to cleanse the liver, while Echinacea boosts the immune system. The plants were all placed on the fabric by hand, making each gown unique.

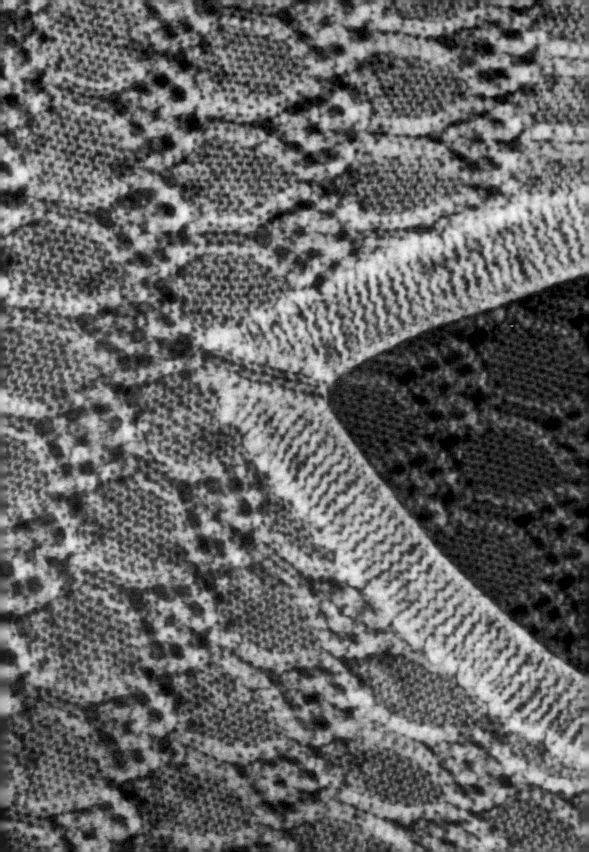

Previous pages, B. Earley
Fabric detail (1:1) from Fleece wrap with photogram print, 1999
Fleece jacket with doily print by Simon Periton, 1997

ANATOMIE DI YÚJÍ

Eley Kishimoto is a husband and wife design duo based in London. They have a confident spontaneous style which readily combines an English street look with a Japanese influence. This is proving a successful mix and their bold printed imagery is recognisable worldwide.

Mark Eley is from south Wales and undertook a B.A. Honours degree in Fashion Textiles Design (Constructed Textiles) with Business Studies at the University of Brighton. Wakako Kishimoto was born in Japan and came to the UK in 1986. She studied at Central Saint Martins College of Art and Design, the London Institute where she specialised in Printed Textiles on the B.A. and M.A. Textile Design for Fashion degrees.

Eley Kishimoto set up their fashion textile design business in 1992 and have supplied leading international designers with playful yet sophisticated textiles. In order to experiment further they decided to launch their own label in 1995. Graphic printing is their signature style and designs are often witty and eye-catching. They are also expert at controlling colour to achieve simple and fresh results. Eley Kishimoto create womenswear with some accessories and also menswear (until 1999). Their fabrics often feature handcraft and reflect the current revival of decorative art skills.

Avant-garde yet commercial, their clothes appeal to young and old alike. Each collection has a theme which is encapsulated by a relevant title. References to garments worn by Kishimoto in her childhood, such as smocking and puffed sleeves appear frequently. Nostalgic imagery, simple cutting and light tailoring suggest a narrative and comment on certain childhood memories. Eley Kishimoto give special consideration to surface interest and texture preferring to work directly with cloth rather than produce paper designs. They are involved in the process from beginning to end – designing, experimenting, sampling, printing and cutting. Fashion designer, Joe Casely-Hayford commissioned textiles from Eley Kishimoto in 1992. Subsequent collaborations include Hussein Chalayan, Clements Ribeiro, Alexander McQueen, Mulligan, Givenchy and Guy Laroche. They now work mainly on the Eley Kishimoto label but continue to work with design houses and textile companies such as Ratti Spa (Italy), World Inc. (Japan), fashion designer, Marc Jacobs and APC. Their most significant commission to date is the Louis Vuitton collaboration for Spring/Summer 2000.

Eley Kishimoto enjoy making connections between the worlds of fashion and art sometimes collaborating with artists and designers from other disciplines. Instead of lavish catwalk shows they reach clientele by making books which feature their clothes, and often work with artists, writers and stylists to complete their vision.

Previous pages, Eley Kishimoto
Fabric detail (1:1) from stickle brick banana dress, spring/summer, 2000
Egg and diamond smock dress, spring/summer, 1998

SHELLYFOX

Felted wool, muslin and burnt elastoplast all feature in garments by Shelley Fox. The designer treats her studio like a laboratory where fabrics are manipulated and tested, often to destruction, with many of the best results coming from happy accidents. There is a mathematical quality to the garments themselves. This is balanced against the wearer's body and it is often impossible to imagine how the clothes will look until they are actually put on the body. The use of high necklines and the positioning of arms and hemline further emphasise the symmetry of the garments.

Developing and customising fabrics is an essential part of Fox's design. Felted wool has been a feature of her work since graduation. The weight of the felt is allowed to impact on the design of the garment as both are developed at the same time. The felt is moulded, layered and stitched. It can also appear scarred from overcooking, or embossed with a pattern. Although it has industrial associations, because of the materials used, it is soft rather than hard. The inherent strength of the material appeals to the designer: "It's a fabric I don't feel precious about when I'm using it. It can withstand a lot, it's so rough and ready and feels like a piece of paper with rough, raw edges".

Many of the fabrics Fox prefers are not traditionally used for fashion garments and instead are sourced from medical and geosynthetic industries. The stretchy elastoplast fabric used in many collections originated in the medical industry. The fabric is transformed by stretching, manipulation, burning and a pattern created by the trail of scorch marks with fabric edges left raw and frayed. Fabrics are further altered by layering transparent and semi-transparent materials. Woven cotton tapestry fabric is allowed to show through a graph design printed on muslin, which in turn is partly covered by yet another translucent layer of fabric.

The patterned and layering of fabric

is used as a counterpoint to the very sculptural forms of the garments themselves. The garments are often based on one or two geometric shapes that are repeated. There is a mathematical reference to be found in the clothing design. This is echoed in the various themes, many of which revolve around communication. Braille and Morse code have inspired collections on a conceptual and graphic level. Braille is used for relief patterns on boiled wool and printed fabrics. The distinctive acoustics of Morse code were used to herald the opening of her Spring/Summer 2000 catwalk show, while the code itself appeared as a graphic pattern on the garments. In one dress the design is printed onto muslin in a pearl powder print process. Another sees a similar design printed on a soft jersey fabric that is brushed to remove part of the print.

Fox's work is marked by an unorthodox approach to both fabric development and pattern cutting. Rules are made, pushed to the edge then broken.

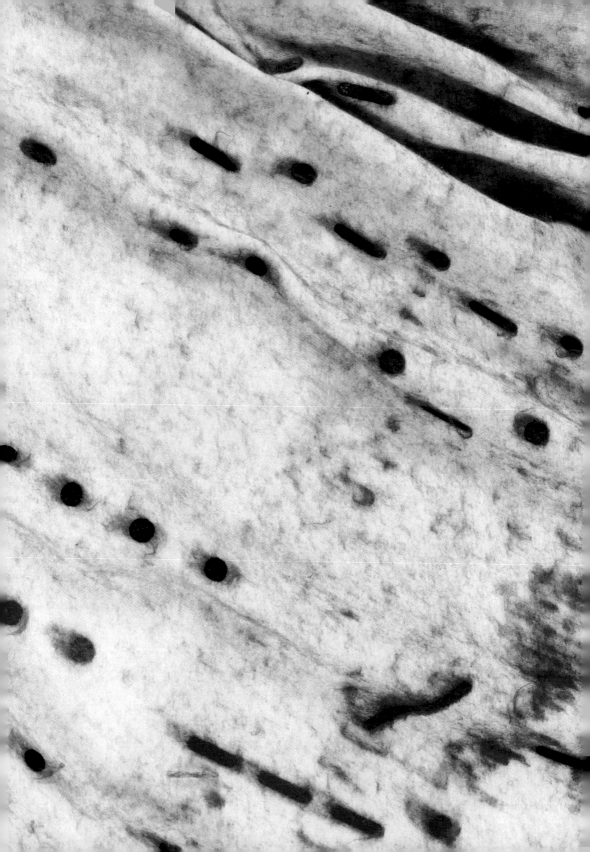

Previous pages, Shelley Fox
Fabric detail (1:1) from Morse code circular dress, 2000
Burnt elastoplast curve dress, 1999

CAROL LEADER

Carol Fraser is a textile/fashion designer who specialises in knitwear for both women and men. Her work is experimental pushing the technical and aesthetic boundaries of knitted textiles for fashion. Her knitwear combines both hand and machine-knitting and often incorporates labour-intensive finishing. Fraser is interested in exploring knitwear techniques to create fashion textiles for others as well as having her own label.

She originally studied Graphics before undertaking a B.A. Honours degree in Printed and Knitted Textiles at Glasgow School of Art. She then specialised further on the M.A. in Fashion Knitwear course at Central Saint Martins College of Art and Design, the London Institute. After graduating in 1993 she set up a knitwear label and became one of the founding members of Commun, a London-based design group and platform for new talent. Fraser collaborated with womens/ menswear designers and created experimental knitwear to complement their work. Commun presented collections from 1993 to 1995 during London Fashion Week in exhibitions throughout the city. In 1995 this group disbanded as people went their separate ways.

In 1994 and 1995, Fraser received New Generation sponsorship which enabled her to stage catwalk shows and static exhibitions as part of London Fashion Week. She has created knitwear for fashion designers such as Fabio Piras (a former member of Commun), Ghost and Jessica Ogden. She was also a design consultant for Artwork. For Ghost, Fraser created complicated knitwear which necessitated a great deal of hand work. One example interpreted a heavily embroidered fabric in a knitted textile using chenille and rayon yarns.

Under her own label Fraser creates knitted textiles, garments and accessories. Inspiration for her collections often comes from investigating traditional craft techniques; she is fascinated with old knitwear patterns, updating them to create a contemporary look. She does not use industrial equipment preferring to knit by hand or use domestic knitting machines which, she considers, allows greater control for the creation of one-off effects. Fraser generally uses natural yarns and buys from British companies. Her intricately detailed knits (both menswear and womenswear) are often embellished by hand, using techniques such as beading, embroidery and the application of sequins. Garment silhouettes are kept simple to emphasise the textile.

Since 1997 Fraser has worked with an agent in Japan for whom she produces a commercial line (accessories and garments) aimed at young Japanese women which is very successful. She also produces fabrics which are sold through agent, Fiona Colquhoun to designers and companies including Donna Karan, Oscar de la Renta and Gap.

Previous pages, Carol Fraser
Fabric detail (1:1) from Fair Isle and lace t-shirt (menswear), 2000
Single sleeve disappearing tartan jacket, 2000

Jo Gordon established a reputation in the mid-nineties with her distinctive hats and more recently with her knitted accessories. She has supplied leading international designers and now creates knitwear and occasional headwear for exhibition.

She grew up in Scotland and trained in Fine Art Sculpture at the Robert Gordon University in Aberdeen. She then went to the Royal College of Art, London and gained her Masters degree in Womenswear Fashion specialising in Millinery. Having first trained in sculpture she approaches hat-making from a different perspective and her graduating collection was impressive with its large-scale feather pieces. This innovative work immediately caught the attention of the press with Browns of South Molton Street, London agreeing to display her hats in their window.

After graduating, Gordon continued to work with a wide range of feathers, transforming their original state by dyeing them various colours and creating new forms. Her sculptural couture hats include wonderfully tiny top-hats, dolphin tails and spirals. She has created headwear for fashion designers including Thierry Mugler, Comme des Garçons, Yohji Yamamoto and Hussein Chalayan.

Based in London she makes accessories for fashion and exhibition. No longer working for fashion designers, Gordon now markets her own knitwear and accessories. For inspiration, she is very interested in period knitting patterns especially from the 1950s. Her contemporary knitwear is simultaneously sophisticated and playful, possessing a nostalgic quality which often makes reference to her childhood holidays on the Scottish islands. Both beautiful and functional, her woollen accessories can withstand diverse weather conditions. She selects the highest quality lambswool or cashmere yarns and enjoys experimenting with unusual combinations of colour. Much of her work has a sculptural quality which refers back to her initial training. Although Gordon creates the designs, the knitting and finishing is completed by specialists in Scotland. The end result is harmonious, fresh, urban and very desirable. Her commercial, ready-to-wear knitwear collections include hats, gloves, ponchos, bags and multi-coloured, striped scarves. These scarves were launched for her Autumn/Winter 1999/2000 collection and have received much favourable publicity.

A recent series of work called Felt Hairstyles shows headwear – a cross between a hat and a hairstyle, simple in form and very eye-catching. Gordon has received New Generation sponsorship and a Crafts Council Start Up Grant. In 1997 her millinery designs were shortlisted for the coveted Jerwood Prize (textiles) and in 1999 she won the Three Bags Full Knitwear Award at the Chelsea Crafts Fair. She regularly shows her work at London Fashion Week.

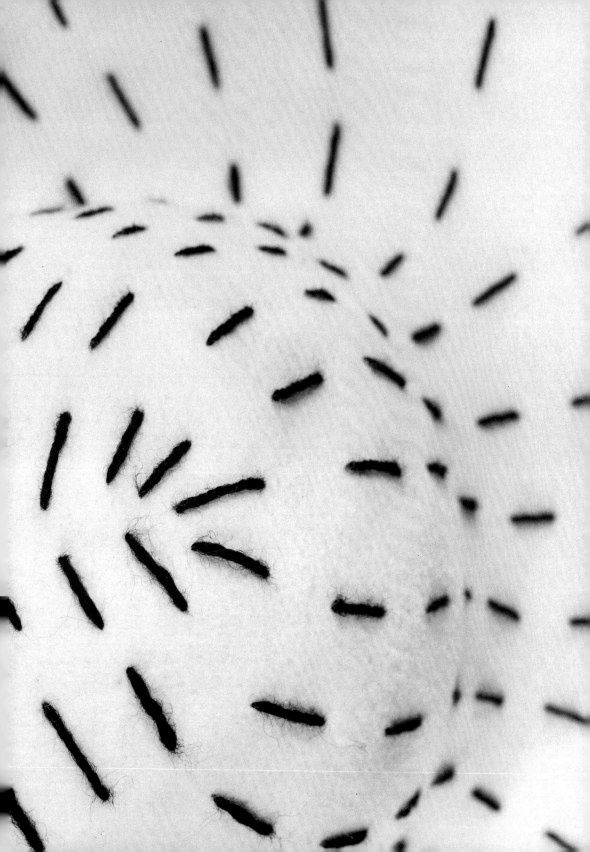

Previous pages, Jo Gordon
Fabric detail (1:1) from felt hairstyle, cream with constrasting black stitching, 2000
Red and orange felt hairstyles, 2000

i.e. uniform combines the talents of fashion designer Roger Lee and textile designer Lesley Sealey. The trademark for their collections is immaculate tailoring with understated fabrics that are printed, beaded and embroidered using hyper-colours.

Lee and Sealey met while studying at the Royal College of Art in London. Sealey spent her final year at college studying print and beading techniques in India. The influence of this remains strong in her work with intricate beading and strong colours a feature in many of i.e. uniform's collections. Lee won a scholarship while at college to undertake a placement at the atelier of Karl Lagerfeld in Paris. His immaculately tailored forms have been a strong influence on the i.e. uniform label, though adopted with a twist. Lee's designs are less formal bringing the London streetstyle influence to bear. Separates dominate each season's collection. This allows the clothes to be combined in different ways in a contemporary 'mix and match' to provide either ultra-glamour or appear understated, depending on how they are mixed and the accessories used. The degree of freedom given to the wearer of their clothes reflects a new form of fashion client who does not want to be a slave to one label but feels free to add elements to create their own individual style.

The garment and textile designs for each collection are developed simultaneously. The inspiration for each collection reflects a liking for contrast and balance. This shows in the style and cut of garment as well as the fabric and finishing treatment. One collection was inspired by modern architecture juxtaposed with a natural environment; another looked to furnishing fabrics and glamour of the 1950s. These ideas do not blend to become one, rather they keep their separate identities in a play on form, texture, colour and surface. Traditional Scottish tartan fabric can be treated with a laser-cut

pattern, while Lurex thread has been laminated to a knitted mohair using a heat process. The fabric treatments were initially developed and produced in-house. Quantities needed and costs are beginning to make this increasingly difficult and i.e. uniform are now developing relationships with manufacturers who can produce fabrics specially for them.

High and low technology are used with equal ease. French knots and beading are used alongside laser-cutting and lamination processes. The base fabrics tend to be purposefully banal in contrast with the finishing treatment which is usually very exuberant and colourful. Jersey, denim, floral cotton and polyester all feature regularly, though unexpected materials also appear. Reflective fabrics, nonwovens, silver and transparent foils are used as trims or to highlight the waist, pocket and hem areas. These are often simply hinted at, almost hidden. It is this subtlety combined with strong sculptural forms that gives i.e. uniform's clothes a style that transcends seasonal collections and gives them a timeless quality.

Previous pages, i.e. uniform
Fabric detail (1:1) from high neck laser-cut sleeveless top, spring/summer 2000
Skirt with beaded flowers and puff sleeve top, autumn/winter 2000

For the label Mulligan, Tracy Mulligan creates refined, contemporary clothing. She works with textile designers who create fabrics featuring print and embroidery.

Mulligan trained in Fashion and Textiles at Central Saint Martins College of Art and Design, the London Institute. In partnership with Barbara Sonnentag, she then formed Sonnentag Mulligan which was successful but unfortunately ceased due to financial problems.

The début solo collection of Mulligan entitled Urban Spiritualist, Autumn/Winter 1998/99 was shown in a London restaurant. Mulligan then received New Generation sponsorship for three subsequent seasons which enabled her to stage catwalk shows and reach an international audience at London Fashion Week.

The look of her clothes is understated with simply-cut and lightly tailored forms. She creates garments which are simultaneously experimental, functional and sophisticated. Eastern and Western influences are apparent with frequent reference to kimonos (kimono wrapping has become her signature), asymmetric draping as well as inspiration taken from French couture. The streamlined silhouettes Mulligan favours, draw attention to the textile which is often embellished. Stating that "surface decoration is the future of fashion" Mulligan expresses interest in handcraft and texture which are employed for both visual and tactile effect. She mixes quality natural fabrics with the latest advances in textile technology to achieve a contemporary look. Mulligan works closely with textile designers who interpret her design influences to create unique fabrics. She has worked with textile design duo, Eley Kishimoto and with textile designer, Karen Nicol.

Mulligan has a strong belief in Eastern spiritual philosophies and each collection has a title taken from the i-ching. Her clothes are also inspired by the world of fine art such as Andy Goldsworthy who directly influenced her first two collections. Other references include the work of Anish Kapoor, Jackson Pollock, Louise Bourgeois, Christo and Jeanne Claude.

Karen Nicol established Karen Nicol Embroidery in 1973 and supplies unique textiles to international fashion designers. She has an embroidery/mixed media textile design group and production studio, while also offering consultancy and analysis of embroidery.

She trained in Embroidery at Manchester Metropolitan University and then studied Textiles at the Royal College of Art, London. Since 1990 she has been course tutor in Embroidery/Mixed Media Textiles at the Royal College of Art. Nicol's main speciality is machine-embroidery including Irish, Cornely, Schiffli and multi-head but also uses beading and hand-embroidery.

Previous pages, Mulligan
Fabric detail (1:1) from dress with string embroidery, autumn/winter, 1999/2000 (textile by Karen Nicol)
Felt coat with gold leaf print, autumn/winter 1998/99 (textile by Eley Kishimoto)

There is a wit and humour to Murray Watson's shoe and boot designs. The forms are exaggerated, almost baroque in their style. They are a popular choice amongst fashion designers for shows and magazine shoots, appearing on the catwalk with Boudicca, Tristan Webber and Robert Carey-Williams. Murray Watson also designs a very different range of shoes for mass production, enjoying the similarities and contrast to be found in the two ways of working. Both use a hand process, although more automation is used for bulk produced shoes designed for high street sales.

Murray Watson's footwear designs are part of, yet outside of fashion. He is most comfortable with leather as his main material, liking the tactile qualities it offers. The colour range and finish are very contemporary, from black and antique brown to clashing colours in shades of bright fuchsia pinks and turquoise. Synthetic trims add to the baroque quality with snakeskin, silk, and nylon contributing further visual and tactile qualities.

Although the styling and choice of heels appears unconventional, there are strong historical precedents for much of this work. Men's straights recall a time when there was not a left and right shoe for men, rather the same shoe or boot was designed to fit both feet. These were by necessity straight. The practice continued until the nineteenth century, although cowboy boots continued to be made in this way for much longer. The contemporary straight by Murray Watson use a cuff-link trim to further emphasise the formality of the earlier shoes and their handmade process.

Ladies lace-up boots with exaggerated heels are reminiscent of Victorian times. The shapes refer to footwear of the era as well as garments that distorted and emphasised the body. The heel of the boot curves beyond the foot's actual heel, effectively reshaping the foot.

The wearer is forced to stand in a quite different posture, with the body shape changing further as they walk. A pair of emerald green boots with a prominent black zip is designed with the zip running around the leg. In a parody on the recent trend for wearing trainers without laces the boots can be worn zipped up, or unzipped to the ankle, falling around the foot.

Heels are the main focus of many of the designs and the source of the designer's humour. Tiny steel cages, BMX bike stands and ice-skating blades are all utilised in different designs. The idea of giving the wearer some decision in the design of their shoe has been taken up by sports footwear companies through the Internet. Murray Watson has designed some footwear with interchangeable heels. Adapted from fittings found in hardware stores, these are given screw attachments for the wearer to change as they choose.

Previous pages, Paul Murray Watson
Fabric detail (1:1) from a pair of green leather boots with spiral black zips, 2000
Pink leather boots with moulded heel for Boudicca, 1999

Hikaru Noguchi creates innovative knitted textiles for fashion, accessories and interiors. Predominantly a knitwear designer, she also designs for woven textiles.

Born in Tokyo, Noguchi initially studied Graphics at Musashino Art University, Tokyo. Coming to the UK in 1989 she studied Constructed Textiles at Middlesex University where she specialised in Knitting. She stayed at Middlesex and undertook a postgraduate year to further her knowledge of textiles, graduating in 1993. In this year she was awarded the Fiona Mackie Prize for Textile Studies by Liberty. After completing her studies, Noguchi chose to remain in London and now has a successful design business.

She has worked for various designers and companies including Matthew Williamson, Kookai and Nicole Farhi and as a design consultant for Habitat, London. She has also undertaken various projects for Barneys, Browns and Paul Smith Women and now produces her own collections.

For the Hikaru Noguchi label she pays great attention to texture and pattern, using bouclé and slub yarns to achieve relief. Shaggy scarves quickly became her signature creation when she teamed them with felted wool jackets or coats in her Autumn/Winter 1994/95 collection. Using quality yarns, such as fine Scottish cashmere she knits by hand as well as utilising Dubied and domestic machines. Whilst the sampling and product finishing take place in her studio, she works closely with factories or home knitters.

Complicated patterning reflects her interest in decoration and she experiments freely with lacy knit and crochet construction techniques. She also draws on traditional British textile crafts such as woven Welsh blankets, Fair Isle knits, Shetland and Arran patterns, updating and interpreting them to create a contemporary look.

Noguchi's garments are both sophisticated yet quirky, especially in their unusual combinations of colour and texture which always harmonise. Inspiration is diverse – from old-fashioned seaside souvenir shops and flea markets to folk textiles such as traditional Japanese cloth and Scottish textile crafts.

She has been awarded New Generation sponsorship which allowed the staging of static exhibitions at London Fashion Week for her Spring/Summer 2000 and Autumn/Winter 2001 collections. This financial help has enabled further experimentation and for her to work with quality fabrics.

Previous pages, Hikaru Noguchi
Fabric detail (1:1) from Fair Isle edge short top with crochet belt, spring/summer, 2000
Welsh blanket jacket with punched leather skirt, autumn/winter, 2000/01

JESSICA OGDEN

Jessica Ogden creates handmade womenswear and accessories by reworking textiles and deconstructing old clothing. Implicit in this position is her rejection of mass production and hard-edged design and her celebration of the individual. Vulnerable and maybe even naive, her collections are also subversive yet sophisticated. Evidence of the hand is considered important in her work which demonstrates a laid-back aesthetic and exudes a certain rawness.

Ogden grew up in Jamaica and her interest in clothes goes back to her childhood there and its diversity of dress. Most of her adult life has been spent in London where she studied Fine Art at London's Byam Shaw before turning to fashion. In 1993 she set up her own label after working for NoLoGo, Oxfam's eco-friendly design collective who recycle clothing. Inspiration is taken directly from collected textiles and clothing; part of the attraction of which is the opportunity it offers to mix various cultural references. The fabrics she chooses are often faded and torn but she quilts, layers, patches and re-stitches them to create unique textiles. She enjoys the romance and sense of history that antique textiles possess. By handcrafting her pieces and making reference to the past she creates a timeless aesthetic which is unaffected by fashion "I see clothes as having a much longer life than a six-month trend". Ogden describes her clothes as being on a journey and having a life of their own – a past, present and future. "I see the fabric I use as having already had a life... I'm just continuing that life. You can read the history: the little pieces of embroidery, the mending, the caring they've received".

Texture and surface interest are paramount, with rare and vintage fabrics often providing good sources. Examples include Toile de Jouy, Madras patchwork, mattress ticking, quilted cloth and antique floral prints. Mixing old and new textiles, she sews them into simple, non-tailored silhouettes such as kimono-styled garments, wrap skirts, pinafore dresses, apron dresses, capes and smocks. In this way her patched, layered and stitched textiles can be shown to advantage.

Ogden's clothes are emotive – because many are sewn by hand, the actual thought process and the making are visible. Not driven by status, her clothes are relaxed, comfortable and tend to work well with existing wardrobes as everyday wear. Her garments, which are bought by young and old alike, break down social barriers by appealing to a wide cross-section of people. Sometimes they may appear second-hand or home-made which is part of her aesthetic, yet Ogden would not object to customers further personalising them.

To coincide with London Fashion Week, September 1998 she displayed an installation, A Dozen Dresses at The Pineal Eye. Glimpse, her Spring/Summer 2000 collection was presented as a mixed media installation including a short film and slide show. This event was staged in an industrial building in London's East End and Ogden collaborated with photographer, Ellen Nolan. In February 2000, she presented an installation called Meander/Wander, for Autumn/Winter 2000/2001 working with photographer, David Hughes and stylist, Lynette Garland.

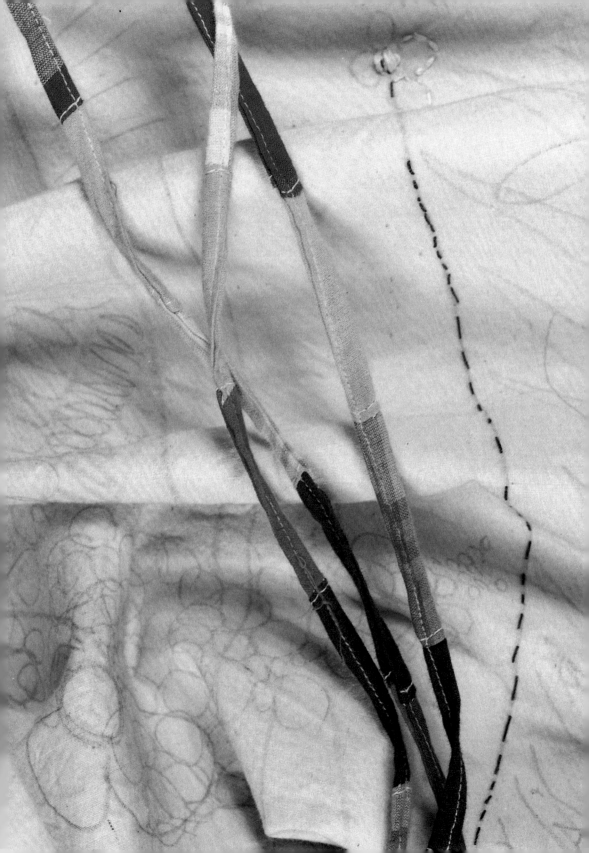

Previous pages, Jessica Ogden
Fabric detail (1:1) from cotton dress. Hand drawing in collaboration with Ellen Nolan, 2000
Two half dresses, one using corduroy Cloth Kit fabric, the other a 1940s printed cotton, 2000

Australian born textile designer Sophie Roet began her career as a trend forecaster with the Li Edelkoort atelier in Paris. She developed new fabrics for the atelier twice a year, during which she discovered her main interest. Having left the University of Brighton she stayed in Paris five years, before returning to study textiles at the Royal College of Art. Roet now works closely with the fashion industry designing textiles for clients who include John Galliano and Alexander McQueen. She is a trend consultant and textile production organiser for Eskandar and has recently launched her own range of scarves.

One of her first clients was fashion designer Hussein Chalayan, who was finishing at the Royal College of Art just as she was starting. He invited her to produce a fabric for his collection. The result was a delicate gossamer-like fabric that was used as an overdress, revealing flashes of light as the under-garment glowed in the dark. The fabric was inspired by Japanese textiles. Roet has visited Japan and finds both contemporary and traditional textile techniques a major source of inspiration: "I think it's their simplicity and the way the use of traditional structures is combined with contemporary yarns. They don't seem to date but somehow transcend time". One of her fabrics has been strongly influenced by hemp kimono fabrics that are referred to as Mizugoromo or Water Cloth. The process involves manipulating the weft yarn like a comb either by hand or using reeds. Some Japanese weavers finely notch the edge of the nail on their middle finger for beating a silk weft. In her interpretation of this process, Roet manipulates the yarn but also uses a devoré finish to create a similar effect. The blue and green fabric is woven using a mix of polyamide monofilament and cotton. The devoré technique removes the cotton to create a fine spider's web effect.

Roet continues to work closely with textile manufacturers in France, Scotland and England. This collaboration began in 1996, when she won the Lea and Bullukian Textile Competition in France. She was recently awarded a commission as part of the Hitec-Lotec project which explores the relationship between craft and industry. Roet saw the commission as an opportunity to produce fabrics that would not be possible in her normal studio environment. She chose to work with technical textile manufacturer Alpha Industrial Laminates and Coatings in Dorset. The company specialise in treating mainly woven glass fibre fabrics for high-performance industrial applications. Her idea was to literally fuse lightweight fashion fabrics with industrial processes, laminating and sandwiching metal and fabric. The company were intrigued by her approach that combined metal sheets with silk, felt and cotton to produce a new series of fabrics using these lightweight and delicate materials.

This combination of industrial and hand processes brings its own aesthetic to the work of Sophie Roet. The fabrics draw different elements together, proving that it is possible to combine traditional craft techniques with the latest industrial technologies.

Previous pages, Sophie Roet
Fabric detail (1:1) from Water, woven nylon monofilament. Fabric length, 1999
Metal textile, aluminum sheeting bonded to cotton. Fabric length, 1999

Adam Thorpe and Joe Hunter comprise Vexed Generation. Their style of menswear is urban streetstyle combined with military apparel. Their choice of fabric is generally high-performance and includes bullet-proof ballistic nylon and smart materials that respond to their environment. The materials are layered, padded and quilted. The design of both clothes and accessories reflect the source of the fabrics in protective applications.

Neither received a conventional fashion or textile design training. Thorpe studied Microbiology at Kingston University, while Hunter attended Middlesex University to study Graphics. They met in London's Portobello Road. At the time Thorpe was working in the music industry and as a sportswear consultant, mainly for Puma. Hunter was involved with a clothing label specialising in recycled clothes. They shared a common interest in social and political issues and decided to use clothing as a means of communication. At the time they met, the Criminal Justice Bill was being debated in parliament attracting media and public attention. Thorpe and Hunter decided to use the bill with its associated issues of civil liberties as a brief for their work. Lacking the technical expertise of pattern-cutting, they decided to take a year out to teach themselves the technical aspects of designing and making garments. This was done mainly through books and manuals. Vexed Generation was launched in 1994.

When asked about the importance of fabric in their work, Hunter's immediate reply was that "Our cloth is as primary as our style. You can't make a shape without having the right cloth". Most of their fabric suppliers produce high-performance technical textiles for military and protective clothing. Over the years they have developed a relationship with these textile manufacturers who view their demands as a challenge. The duo are behind many of the textile innovations we have seen in recent years such as Teflon coated denim, resin impregnated

polyamide and the use of ballistic nylon for non-military applications. Their work with the fabric does not end with manufacturing and finishing treatments but extends to garment cutting and assembly. Textiles are often layered and quilted for reasons of aesthetics as well as performance. A layered fabric from Vexed might include a liner of Outlast and an outer layer of ballistic nylon, providing protection to the wearer from climate changes and gunfire. Outlast uses a micro-encapsulation technique to incorporate a Phase Change Material (PCM) that has the ability to change its state depending on temperature. Outlast is more usually used in sportswear or protective clothing to provide the wearer with their own climate-controlled environment, keeping them warm in winter and cool in summer.

Vexed Generation are keen to establish that their work is not just about social issues. They are happy to provide interesting shapes with new solutions, usually in the form of fabric innovation. Comfort is important, as they believe their clothes should be comfortable to wear, regardless of seasons or climate changes. This is not unlike the performance demanded by protective and military clothing specifications so it is no surprise that many of their fabrics should originate from the same source.

Previous pages, Vexed Generation
Fabric detail (1:1) from padded trousers with Teflon coating on denim, 2000
Hooded shock jacket, ballistic nylon, neoprene and outlast phase change material, 1997

NIGEL ATKINSON

1964	Born
1982–83	Portsmouth College of Art, foundation course
1983–86	Winchester School of Art, BA Textiles
1987	Established hand printing workshop in London
1991	Expanded premises to Camden Square
1994	Launched Nigel Atkinson Accessories
1996	Florence Biennale, Italy, Museo dell'Opifio delle pietre dure
1997	Launched Nigel Atkinson Interior Textiles

List of works

01	Six tier, hand-embroidered satin organza wrap, 2000 *Embroidered by Bengali craftsmen*
02	Cotton organdie/silk tulle layered wrap, 2000 *Hand-dyed and layered*
03	Embroidered chrysanthemum dressing-gown, 2000 *Hand printed cotton gauze interprets embroidery*
04	Sea anemone dressing-gown, 2000 *Hand-printed velvet achieves a contoured effect*
05	Sea anemone dressing-gown, 2000 *Hand-printed cotton gauze gives an embossed look*

01   02   03   04

1961	Born in Sri Lanka
1976	Moved to London
1982	Started Architecture degree
1989–92	Edinburgh College of Art, BA in Printed Textiles
1994–97	Royal College of Art, London, MPhil in nonwoven 3D textiles
1997	Moulded headwear worn on Chanel's catwalk show, Paris autumn/winter
1998–99	Collaborated with Boudicca on their spring/summer collections
1999–01	Loughborough University, PhD, textiles in collaboration with the Engineering department

   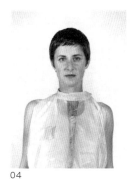

01   02   03   04

HUSSEIN CHALAYAN

1970	Born in Cyprus
1991–93	Central St Martins, BA (Hons) in Fashion
1994	Cartesia, first solo exhibition, West Soho Galleries, London
1994	Temporary Interference, sponsored by Jigsaw, shown in Japan
1995	Winner of Absolut Vodka award
1996	Jam – style music, and media, Barbican Gallery, London
1997	The Cutting Edge, Victoria and Albert Museum, London
1998	Addressing the Century; 100 years of art and fashion, Hayward Gallery, London
1999	British Fashion Awards, Designer of the Year
1999	Visions of the Body; Fashion or Invisible Corset, Kyoto Costume Institute
1999	Echoform exhibition toured to San Francisco, Vienna, New York
1999	Costumes for Handel's Messiah, New York
1999	British Fashion Awards, Designer of the Year

List of works

01	Buried dress, S/S 1995 *Silk, buried in soil to achieve distressed look*
02	Pixellated print dress, S/S 1996 *Silk, fabric design Eley Kishimoto*
03	Architecture series (4 dresses), S/S 2000 *Cotton, fabric design b consultants*
04	Printed skirt and top, A/W 2000 *Corduroy*
05	Flock print series (3 dresses), A/W 1997 *Cotton*

01

02

03

04

05

1970 Born Rebecca Earley
1992–94 Central St Martins, distinction in Fashion
1993 Established her own label of printed textiles, called B. Earley
1994 Street Style, Victoria and Albert Museum, London
1995 New Faces, Victoria and Albert Museum, London
1995 Sarah Staton's Supastore, Manchester and Bristol
1996 Revelations, The Barbican, London
1996 The Subterraneous SS, Clink St Gallery, London
1996 New Generation award, British Fashion Council
1996 No Picnic, Crafts Council, London
1997 Textile Diversity, Glasgow School of Art
1998 Hyperhall, Øksnehallen, Copenhagen
1998 The New Liberty, London College of Fashion
1999 Peugeot Awards, Textile winner
2000 Means of production, award from London Arts Board

01 Lace dress, 1994
Polyester microfibre. Heat photogram print
02 Pin-stripe trouser-suit, 1995
Satin finish synthetic. Heat photogram print with pins laid on fabric by hand
03 Doily print jacket, 1997
Recycled soda bottle fleece with heat photogram print. Doily pattern by sculptor Simon Periton
04 Fleece wrap, 1999
Recycled soda bottle fleece with heat photogram print
05 Healing herbs series, 1999
Satin backed brushed polyester microfibre. Breast cancer radiotherapy treatment gown. Commissioned by the Public Art Commissions Agency 1999
06 Gypsophila dress, 2000
Cotton/polyester with heat photogram print

01   02   03   04

05   06

ELEY KISHIMOTO

Mark Eley and Wakako Kishimoto
comprise Eley Kishimoto

1965   Wakako Kishimoto born Japan
1986–92 Fashion/Print at Central St Martins

1968   Mark Eley born Wales
1986–90 Fashion/Weave at University of Brighton

1992   Established Eley Kishimoto label
1992–   Clients for whom they have designed textiles include
Joe Casely-Hayford, Sonja Nuttall, Antonio Berardi,
Hussein Chalayan, Jil Sander, Yves St Laurent and
Alexander McQueen

List of works

01   Astrakhan coat, A/W 1996/7
Printed polyamide interprets astrakhan. Rainwear
02   Egg and diamond smock dress, S/S 1998
Devoré printed cotton. Cruise
03   Cake suit, A/W 1998/99
Hand printed on knitted lambswool. Cake
04   Shrink printed top and broken check printed
skirt, S/S 1999
Notes
05   Stickle brick banana dress, S/S 2000
Pigment printed cotton. Work
06   Flower shoulder print batwing top and flower
stripe skirt. Matching boots, A/W 2000/01
Librarians Day Off

01

02

03

04

05

06

1965   Born
1993–96   Central St Martins, MA in Fashion and Textiles
1997   Launched her own label
1998   No Picnic, Crafts Council, London
1999   Best of Spring/Summer 99, The Design Museum,
            London
1999   Peugeot Design Awards, finalist, London
1999   Winner of Jerwood Fashion Prize, London
1999–01   Lost and Found, British Council touring exhibition in
            Frankfurt, Warsaw, Belgium, Bordeaux and Stockholm
2000   Language of Fashion, British Council, Lithuania
2000   Fashion in Motion, Victoria and Albert Museum, London

List of works

01

02

03

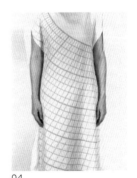
04

05

06

07

CAROL FRASER

List of works

01	Safety pin and embroidered dress, 2000
	Hand and machine knitted with decoration
02	Single sleeve disappearing tartan jacket, 2000
	Machine knitted
03	Crazy line sweater, 2000
	Hand and machine knitted
04	Broomstick crochet and sequin sweater (menswear), 2000
	Hand crocheted and knitted with decoration
05	Fair Isle and Lace t-shirt (menswear), 2000
	Hand knitted and embroidered
06	Beaded whirlpool vest (menswear), 2000
	Hand crocheted with applied beading

01

02

03

04

05

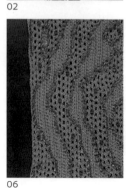

06

1967	Born
1993–95	Royal College of Art, London, MA Womenswear, Fashion
1996	New Generation award
1996	Objects of Our Time, Crafts Council London and New York
1997	Jerwood Prize for Textiles (nominee), Crafts Council, London
1997	The Cutting Edge, Victoria and Albert Museum, London
1997	Best of British Design, Cologne Design Museum
1998	Satellites of Fashion, Crafts Council, London and touring abroad

List of works

01   Felt hairstyle, 2000
        Bright red felted wool is formed and cut
02   Felt hairstyle, 2000
        Bright orange felted wool is formed and cut
03   Felted hairstyle, 2000
        Yellow felted wool is formed and cut
04   Felted hairstyle, 2000
        Black felted wool is formed and cut
05   Felt hairstyle, 2000
        Pink felted wool is formed and cut
06   Felt hairstyle, 2000
        Cream felted wool is formed cut and stitched in black

01

02

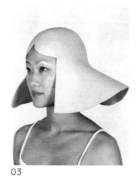

03

04

05

06

I.E. UNIFORM

Roger Lee and Lesley Sealey comprise i.e. uniform

1970	Roger Lee born
1991–94	Kingston University, BA Womenswear
1994–96	Royal College of Art, London, MA Fashion (Womenswear)

1971	Lesley Sealey born
1989–92	Nottingham Trent University, BA Textiles
1993–96	Royal College of Art, London, MA Textiles

1997	i.e. uniform established
1999–00	New Generation award
2000	First catwalk show, Atlantis 2 Gallery, East London

List of works

01 High neck laser-cut top and shorts, S/S 2000
Top in floral cotton print with laser-cut pattern and aluminised fabric lining. Denim shorts with net hem

02 Jacket and panel skirt, S/S 2000
*Jacket in floral cotton print with mesh layer
Skirt with glitter print*

03 Day-glo top and skirt, S/S 2000
Synthetic top and industrial cream denim skirt with embroidery and reflective fabric details

04 Glitter t-shirt and pleated skirt, S/S 2000
Jersey t-shirt with glitter print. Floral cotton and mesh layer skirt

05 Sleeveless top and skirt, A/W 2000
Cotton skirt and pointelle jersey top

06 Puff sleeve top and beaded skirt, A/W 2000
Suiting fabric skirt with beading, pointelle jersey top

01

02

03

04

05

06

1962   Born Tracy Mulligan
1985–87   Chelsea College of Art and Design
1987–90   Central St Martins, BA in Fashion and Textiles
1998   Established Mulligan label and first solo collection
1998   New Generation award for Walking Your Path collection
1999   Nominated for British Fashion Design Awards
1999   New Generation award for Clarity collection

01

02

03

04

05

06

PAUL MURRAY WATSON

1968	Born
1993–95	Cordwainers College, London, handsewn shoe course
1997	Designed shoes for Tristan Webber
1998	Designed shoes for Boudicca
1999	Designed shoes for Robert Carey-Williams and Boudicca
1999	First collection show at London Fashion Week
2000	Designed shoes for Lizzy Disney, New York

List of works

01   Moulded heel boots (7 pairs), 1999
Leather. Designed for Boudicca
02   Ankle boot with ice-skate heels, 1998
Leather
03   Men's straights, 1999
Leather with cuff-link clasps
04   Spiral boots, 1999
Leather with steel caged heel
05   Spiral shoe, 1999
Leather with steel caged heel
06   Silver evening shoes, 1999
Leather with metal wall hook heels
07   Ankle boots with assorted heels, 1999
Leather with heels including a silver hand grenade and BMX stand fitting

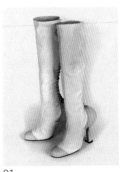
01

01

02

03

04

05

06

07

1967	Born in Japan
1985–88	Musashino Art University, Tokyo, degree in Visual Communication
1989–93	Middlesex University, Constructed Textiles
1992–93	Sembikiya Gallery, Tokyo
1996	Objects of Our Time, Crafts Council, London and New York
1994	Sembikiya Gallery, Tokyo
1998	Satellites of Fashion, Crafts Council, London and touring abroad

List of works

01   Fair Isle edge top and punched leather skirt with crochet belt, S/S 2000
Machine knitted top, punched leather fringed skirt and hand-crocheted belt

02   Mexican yoke dress, S/S 2000
Machine knitted garment with colouring detailing

03   Welsh blanket jacket, A/W 2000/2001
Woven wool with fringed edging

04   Welsh blanket jacket, A/W 2000/01
Woven wool with fringed edging

01   02   03   04

JESSICA OGDEN

1970	Born in Jamaica
1987	Rhode Island School of Design, USA, foundation course
1988	Moved to London
1988–92	Byam Shaw, London, Fine Art
1993	Established her own label
1998	Pineal Eye, London
1999–01	Lost and Found, British Council touring exhibition in Frankfurt, Warsaw, Belgium, Bordeaux and Stockholm
1999	Glimpse, East London during London Fashion Week
2000	Meander/Wander, collaboration with David Hughes and Lynette Garland, Studio Sienko, London

List of works

01	Antique fabric dress, S/S 1998
Pleated and appliquéd fabrics
02	Antique fabric skirt and cape, A/W 1999
Antique and old dishcloth fabrics with hand stitching and embroidery
03	Two half dresses, S/S 2000
One using an old dish cloth fabric, the other a cotton fabric featuring a drawing collaboration with Ellen Nolan
04	Two half dresses, S/S 2000
One using cloth kit fabric, the other a 1940s printed cotton
05	Backless antique fabric top and denim skirt, A/W 2000
Quilted antique fabrics and denim
06	Hand drawing on dress, S/S 2000
Drawing collaboration with the photographer Ellen Nolan. Embroidery detail on cotton

01

02

03

04

05

06

1969	Born in Australia
1988–89	Central St Martins, foundation course
1989–91	University of Brighton, BA in Woven Textile Design
1993–95	Royal College of Art, London, MA in Woven Textile Design
1994	Winner of Woven Textile Designer prize for Texprint, Interstoff, Frankfurt
1996–	Clients include John Galliano, Alexander McQueen, Gianni Versace, Georgina von Etzdorf
1998–	Textile consultant to various textile companies including Eskandar, Christiano Verger, Milan and Cotonificio Albini, Bergamo
1997	Textile consultant to Nicole Farhi, London
1998	Museum of Textiles, Toronto

01	Oyster Shell, 1998
	Silk, polyamide and viscose fabric length.
	In loom state the fabric is flat, but crazes
	when washed in warm water
02	Water, 1999
	Woven nylon monofilament. Fabric length.
	Selected by Eskandar for scarves
03	Chinese, 1999
	Woven wool/silk with cotton cord piping.
	Fabric length commissioned by Eskandar for garments
04	Metal textile, 1999
	Aluminium sheeting bonded to cotton.
	Fabric length developed for Hitec/Lotec commission
05	Broken Line, 2000
	Silk hand-woven textile length
06	Shadow, 2000
	Woven wool with cashmere finish. Shawl

01   02   05

VEXED GENERATION

Adam Thorpe and Joe Hunter
comprise Vexed Generation

1967	Joe Hunter born
1986–89	Middlesex University, London, Graphics
1969	Adam Thorpe born
1988–91	Kingston University, Microbiology
1994	Vexed Generation label established
1995	First store established in London's Soho
1998	Powerhouse, UK, London
1999	Inner City Pressure, National Gallery, Prague
1999	Fastforward, Kunsthaus, Vienna
1999	Lost and Found, British Council touring exhibition to Frankfurt, Warsaw, Belgium, Bordeaux and Stockholm

List of works

01 Ballaneck top and padded trousers,
    A/W 1998, A/W 1995
    Wool and microfibre top and Teflon coated denim padded trousers.
02 Shock jacket, A/W 1998, A/W 1995
    Ballistic nylon, neoprene and Outlast phase change material
03 Shopper bag, A/W 1997
    Cordura and airflow foam liner
04 Wrap liberation jacket, A/W 1998
    Cordura and airflow foam liner
05 Ladies gathered top and skirt, S/S 1998
    Cordura and wicking fabric
06 Ballaneck jacket, A/W 1998
    Neovelvet

01

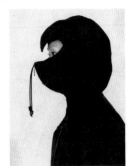
02

03

04

Published by The British Council
10 Spring Gardens London SW1 2BN
to coincide with the launch of the
international tour at the Crafts Council
Gallery London 8 November 2000 –
14 January 2001

The
British
Council

ISBN 0 86355 462 8

© The British Council 2000
Text © copyright the authors
Photographs © copyright Michael Danner

Exhibition curated by
Sarah Braddock and Marie O'Mahony

Exhibition organised by Louise Wright
and Jo Gutteridge

Exhibition designed by
dlm & b consultants

Publication edited by
Brett Rogers

Photographs styled by
Samantha Perry

Catalogue and typeface designed by
A2-GRAPHICS/SW/HK

Printed by BAS, Over Wallop

www.fabricoffashion.co.uk

Special mention and thanks to

Andrea Rose, Visual Arts, The British Council
Frédérique Dolivet and Hannah Hunt, Visual Arts, The British Council
The designers and their studio assistants
Michael Danner and Ulrike Leyens
Craig Henderson and the British Council workshop
Louise Taylor, Louise Pratt, Jane Thomas, Crafts Council, London
Misako Imahori and Laura Jones (models)
Annika McVeigh, Chalayan studio
Nick Barley
Tom Barker, Richard Harrison (b consultants)
Oliver Domeisen, Jee Eun Lee, Michelle Mambourg (dlm)